A Good Caddie Is Hard To Find

by

Schulz

CollinsPublishersSanFrancisco

A Division of HarperCollins*Publishers*

Tee
Time!

Birdies,
Bogies &
Sand Traps

卌 卌

A Good
Caddie Is
Hard To Find

IF IT GETS TOO HEAVY, WE CAN ALWAYS TAKE OUT THE TEES..

A Packaged Goods Incorporated Book
First published 1996 by Collins Publishers San Francisco
1160 Battery Street, San Francisco, CA 94111-1213
http://www.harpercollins.com
Conceived and produced by Packaged Goods Incorporated
276 Fifth Avenue, New York, NY 10001
A Quarto Company

Library of Congress Cataloging-in-Publication Data
Schulz, Charles M.
[Peanuts. Selections]
A good caddie is hard to find / by Charles Schulz.
p.   cm.
ISBN 0-00-225203-1
I. Title
1996
741.5'973—dc20   96-17750
CIP

Printed in Hong Kong

1 3 5 7 9 10 8 6 4 2

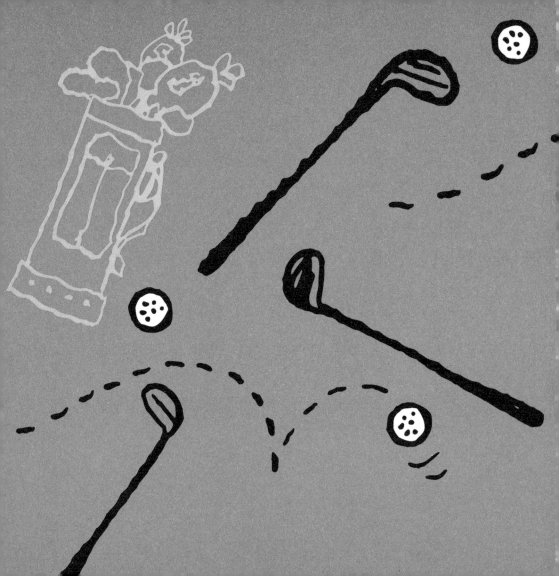